Field Of Chaos

Thomas Barbalet

Tom Barbalet, Elands, Summer 1993.

Introduction

This text was written by me on an original green-screen x86
computer squirreled away in my mother's house at the end of
1993. It represented an attempt to frame what was a series of
troubling experiences. I have decided just to publish the Elands
part of my writing because it shows if this was what I was willing
to do, what had my former life been like?

There is something unique in this text. Not only was this written
by me in 1993, it was edited by my mother in 2023. My mother
features in the book too.

This left me with a great sense of peace that this writing was an
acknowledgement that the experiences were important.

Tom Barbalet, May 26, 2024.

Field Of Chaos

Chapter 1

A story about a holiday, an existence in December, 1993.

I was seventeen.

There was nothing like a good church service with a good sermon. Church, St Pauls, Manuka, Anglican, was so unfathomably different to any other weekly experience I had, that it almost disguised the week of petty propaganda "empowerment" that gave me nothing but a sickly sense that I was just a tool.
Almost, but not completely.
Re-education (schooling) was to me a lot like a prison sentence where the jailer had thrown the key, just slightly more than you could reach from the cell. So I could see the key, I just couldn't get to it. I was alienated from my school peers - an alienation I had created - yet to the outside world it was clear that I had to be one of them because we were all compressed in the same mess. In my previous novella I had created a description of reality which had slightly twisted my outlook. It was my assignment in a re-education institution that both I and my character from the novella shared.

Then came the summer holidays, summer holidays where I, Australia's last surviving, anti-viral-software-creator could travel elsewhere to find companionship.

The place was Elands, northern New South Wales.

I had never been there, but my friend, Alex, had. He and I were going to travel to this northern location to reconnect with our friend Unknown, who we had met the year before. Unknown had lived with Alex, in Alex's parents" home in comfortable Manuka, and so a deep friendship was formed between Alex and Unknown, and a secondary friendship between Unknown and me.

I was lured to Elands with the thought of teaching people about polymorphism and the various disciplines that surrounded it. It was going to be a holiday! I would not have to think about school or re-education institutions or any of the previous year. This was a time of relaxation and quiet thought, perhaps even working on another book.

The morning began at 6.45 am, a little late for a 7.20 am departure. But somehow my mother, twin brothers and I left at 7.45 am, to collect Alex from the next suburb over, leafy Manuka, and travel to the Canberra Railway Station. The bus arrived exactly at 8.22am and Alex and I boarded, with much saying goodbye from family.

But now we were off on the adventure, as cliched as that was. I had slept very little the night before. I had seen Alex in the afternoon, his excitement invariably rippled from his body. He had traveled to Elands before, in April 1993, and he knew it was the Eden of Australia, bar the fact that there were leeches, but I guess that just pointed to the fact that we were still Earthbound. As I wrote in my notebook we traveled through Collector, a small country town, and then on through Goulburn, the perfect example of a large country town, complete with bearded old ladies who smoked cigarettes out on their lawns and glared angrily at our CountryLink coach. Burger Rings is what we ate. The bus was only a quarter full, so we each could easily sit in double seats.

All was good.

The Great Dividing Range changed again and yet again as the bus moved from Canberra to Sydney. It certainly made you think about existence - every single organism had a different existence.

We reached the outskirts of Sydney, at 11.30am and although we had lived and breathed Canberra for most of our existence, now we traveled on, to another existence. Through places like Punch-bowl and Strathfield. Through the fenced reservoir system and a fellow called ABUSE, who wrote his name on walls. And past the Aston Circus, complete with elephants and camels; they wouldn't let them into Canberra - a ban on Circus animals.

We were half an hour early! Four hours in Sydney went remarkably quickly. An hour was devoted to the purchasing of an extremely dubious hot meal, Alex ordering a chicken roll, I ordered 'a' fried rice and we both had a 'Chinese roll'. We went on to Belmore park to consume our food. After eating and feeding the pigeons a majority of the rice and chicken roll, we moved on to Chinatown where we purchased some cola consumables and moved back through our now familiar park. Back to a walkway, where we met a Jehovah's Witness, who took an hour and a half.

With an hour and a half remaining we purchased a copy of the FACE (October, 1993) and wandered around central Sydney.

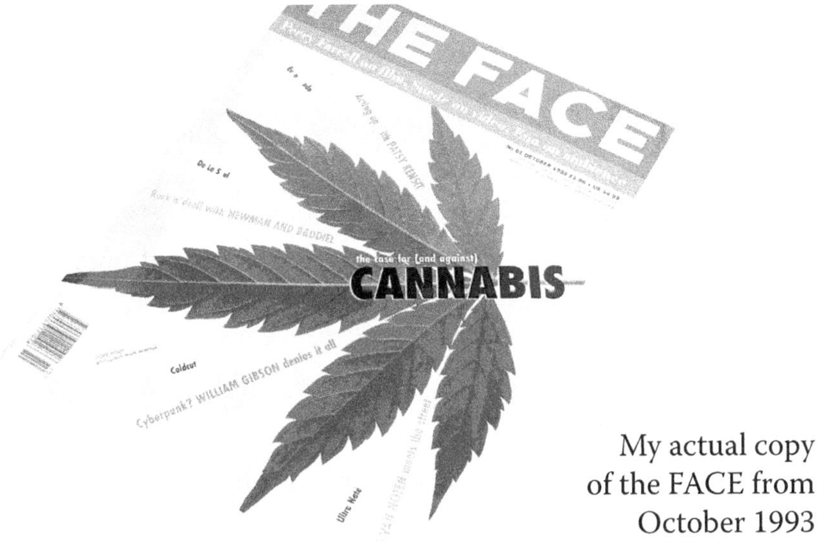

My actual copy
of the FACE from
October 1993

Returning to the station, Alex began reading a version of my novella. The only problem was that it wasn't too well edited and there were many glaring errors. It was an interesting discussion piece, and Alex spent much time arguing about semantics and pointing out the glaring errors - your author was illiterate. My initial worries about the trip, for I had a few, was about conforming to the feral genre. But traveling with Alex, I found I could tolerate the occasional exclamation of 'fuck' and 'festy bong-water', not to mention well-worn clothes and an odor, actually induced by the flu but similar to not showering for weeks.

This was the first time I had no backing out option in these mysterious adventures and no matter what happened, it was sixteen days and fifteen gorgeous nights in beautiful Elands. It was a bit like a commando novel, where they dropped you in the middle of a war zone and came back in sixteen days to pick you up. The explanation of the pre-arrival situation was something like this: Alex had traveled to Elands with his friend, Martin. Unknown had lived with Alex, so as one might imagine Unknown and Alex were pretty good friends. Martin, however, did not know Unknown, and caused 'considerable stress' while he was there, according to Alex. This meant that Alex had not really left the 'property' for fear that Unknown's friends and relations would meet Martin.

To explain another aspect of our predicament, you need to understand that Alex and my only communication with Unknown came throughan answering machine. The answering machine was very familiar to Alex and me, seeing we each called it many times to try and confirm that we were actually going to get picked up at the station close to Elands. We had received only one message from Unknown which came through a conversation Unknown had with my mother.

The message was to call him back, but after many calls and just getting the same message from the answering machine we had now traveled six hundred kilometers on the basis of a two minute conversation. It was extremely irrational, but that was all part of the adventure and chaos of life. Escapism, I told myself: escapism was the basis of the feral genre. One must be slow getting into high level conspiracist hacking tales.

There were so many, and I knew Unknown would want to hear them all, preferably more than once - so he could retell them at a later date. Each time I retold them I would need to re-emphasize some sections. Although Unknown was cannabis and C2H5OH hardened, he still had surface - real - emotions. Which is something Alex and I lacked.

We arrived at Wingham station - after spending five hours in a carriage with Sydney private school girls who spent the whole evening singing chart songs.

By this point, both Alex and I had the sickly sensation that we could be spending an evening at the train station because Unknown hadn't actually listened to the answering machine. The train station was the hot and happening place to be on a Sunday evening - even the station guard had gone home. Alex and I pooled our stuff together - a majority of which was mine - on a bench and proceeded to walk over to the car park and wait for a sign of life. We didn't really know what we were looking for - a car, any car, of any description; and apart from this, the car could have been driven by anyone - so that made the options pretty open. We noticed a car pulling up opposite the train station. This had to be Unknown. We assumed he could drive by now. But it turned out to be a party on the other side of the road. Alex walked over and introduced himself. I was rather more hesitant and guarded the bags.

Cautiously, like a young pup, I edged towards the beer drinking crowd.

"This is Tom," Alex introduced me. There were two early twenty year old males sipping Victoria Bitters one wearing blue overalls and the other wearing a red flannel shirt. Attached to each where two similarly classed females.

"We're going to Elands," Alex said. "Do any of you guys know a bloke called Unknown?"

"Oh, he's doing Engineering at Newcastle? Isn't he?" the first man asked.

"No, just a mechanics course," Alex laughed.

A small blue Suzuki minivan pulled up and a woman called out, "Are you Alex and Tom?"

I looked at Alex, Alex smiled back - we were going to Elands! "So who's who?"

"I'm Alex, and he's Tom," This woman was Unknown's mother, and the wife of Cyber-Shaman. She was a very rugged, very nice person - what else did I expect? The journey of about 23 miles took an hour and a half. The conversation was pretty relaxed. Unknown had been out in the forest, which was an area called Compartment 209 - they had a logging blockade.

You got the feeling that you were being couriered into an army camp moving from one existence, one of middle class suburbia, to another, a jungle warfare camp - but we weren't, this was just Elands, home of the cyber-hippies, and as we bumped along the never ending misty dirt road and heard stories of the eternal downpour that had occurred merely hours ago, we worked our way up an ever-steep mountain.

We arrived at 'block 5' just before midnight, and walked through the dark rain drenched trail to the main building. The main building was a three level (lowest level underground) erection that could not have been built anywhere else. It was a composite of solid timber and offcut brick. It offered a comfortable stay, although it wasn't middle class suburbia.

"Ah, a clean Cyber-Shaman," Unknown's mother exclaimed on seeing her spouse walk in with wet hair.

I met the main building's dog, Bunya, a small golden bitzerdog and slept on a mattress. Alex slept in the loft which was only about twelve square feet, and five feet above my head. The evening concluded with me sipping a cup of warm milky tea.

Chapter 2

I awoke to begin a letter, and explored the four meters I could see around the building - it was very foggy. I got the sense that I was entering something that was bigger than I expected. Alex slowly awoke, and came down the ladder to greet a figure walking towards the building - I could not identify him.

"Ah, man, we got in last night."

"So I heard," said the figure - who had to be Forrest, Unknown's brother.

"This is Tom."

"Hi," I said, raising my hand in a tribute signal.

"I heard you got in last night. Unknown's just waking up - perhaps you would like to see him." So we followed Forrest's skinny figure fifty meters, along a brick-paved track to a caravan. The door of the caravan swung open to uncover a slight, lightly bearded host, Unknown who had just woken up.

"Ah, Alex - and it's good to see you made it, Tom."

"It was difficult!"

"Yeah, imagine so. I've just been in the forest. I got there and the W.F.A. people - you've heard of W.F.A.? - it is an acronym, Wingham Forest Action - they are involved with the forest protection. They try to say that they are just the legal and media workers, but they have control of the forest movement. So I turned up, and those dumb hippies don't have a clue. Never trust a bloody hippy!" Unknown laughed.

"Yeah, you know." He wobbled one hand.

"So I turned up there and they just don't have a clue! There was a camp full of sick people and the old women wanted to work in the rain. And there are sick people in the camp, they had some intestinal disorder - a parasitic infection - really sick, they couldn't do anything. And these fools want to move out and do recon in the rain - with sick people in the camps! Never trust a bloody hippy!" He laughed again. "These old women, they are real bitches - so they insist that they are off doing really important recon, and I am back in the camp, and these fucking hippies don't even want to build a fire. So they left me there and the only shelter was filled with really sick people - all over the ground," he signaled with his hands. "They left me to build a fire and boil all the water and clean all the utensils - because the sick people were just passing the illness on. So - I had worked for two days, without sleep, but I'm used to that - so I built a fire, by pushing all the sick people and finding the dry kindling under the ground sheet. And then these fucking hippies, the fucking old women, come back to camp and say to me, "Well, Unknown, if you aren't going to do anything you can go back. And I felt like just turning around and punching one of them. But I thought, fuck these stupid hippies - I'll leave these stupid bitches, because that's what they were, stupid hippy bitches. So I came back here and I hadn't slept for four days, and just crashed."

He reached over and picked up a guitar and played a tune, that I will call the Elandian Revolutionary Tune - (F, G#, F, D#, C, F, G#, F, D#, C, D, C, D#, C. Not a great tune.)

After playing this a few times, we moved out of Forrest's caravan.

My first vision of Elands in light was a two and a half kilometer wander to the Elands General Store. Unknown had begun on an explanation of why W.F.A.'s radio scanner was so illegal. It was all about the Communications Act of 1914 - the same law that governed hacking. Ironically I knew the law and its implementation well and could even quote sections verbatim. It apparently was okay to listen to a scanner that picked up a 'secret' or 'secure' channel, it was just the process of communicating this information that produced the illegality.

Of course this kind of tale led directly into a somewhat stammered early 1993 hacking tale, which featured those classic tale-getters, which was described in the first half of my previous novella. I was rather tired of re-telling the same tales. Wasn't this the reason I had written the classic Conspiracy? The telling of the tales caused me no enjoyment and it really could have been likened to a piece of poorly cooked chicken - after consuming it - all you wanted to do was expel it from your body. My tales wouldn't attract anyone - if anything they repelled all comers - and I was beginning to doubt if I could use them as a money earner. But I had a duty to tell them! After all, it showed the fact that I had an ultra-black reality which meant that even if I wasn't feral, they - the people at elands - would still give me support because I was just another brother from the Anti-System. (I omitted the fact that I had actually worked with Defence, the government briefly as well: we couldn't have an Anti-System defector in our camp!)

And the fact that although I had received some death threats, I was, down in my soul, still a middle class cultured idiot who detested excessive drug and alcohol use. This assumption was the logical one, just not the right one.

We walked to 'the Elands General Store', Unknown had turned eighteen two days before and with his passport as identification he was going to purchase some liquor from the store. This was obviously a big moment, he could now destroy his brain legally. We were also planning on purchasing food as well as intoxicating fluids. Elands General Store was unbelievable, it was virtually unstocked, there were gaps in the shelves and all the items lay unpriced. Alex homed in on the chocolate biscuits.

"Fellas, when you get to be my age, you look for something more solid," Unknown said, mustering up the most aged voice he could possibly find. This amused me a little, as much as one would imagine. Unknown purchase some overproof rum, and two bottles of THE brand-name cola. Alex and I waved through the dry cracker biscuits, bought two packets, a three hundred gram unit of cheese, a cut of salami, a bottle of ginger beer and a lime fizz concoction.

The day was spent meeting locals and watching The Simpsons - a familiar hobby - at a place called 'Jezz's', one of Unknown's neighbors. The television was to be found in another neighbor's civilized brick house, which had such luxuries as a toilet, taps (fresh running water). And it wasn't rotting. The 'owner' of the house was a beautiful white and ginger soft-paw (cat), that had developed a very swanky walking movement and enjoyed getting itself stuck in the cupboards.

We returned to the main building, a one and a half kilometer walk and Unknown talked about the crossbow and then about the commune's plane. The plane dated back to when he was in Canberra. It was used for aerial recon work. It was light, maneuverable, remotely and computer controlled, and would cost a fortune - but that didn't matter, it was a dream - and what were humans without dreams - I believe they were called anti-viral-software-creators! Unknown, Forrest, Alex and I moved on to Brian's house. Brian Cyber-Shaman's son, was not in residence.

It wasn't clear where he was, but to use his computer, we had to do work on his shack. This was primarily through laying pavers. The problem was that it was raining continuously and this meant it was impossible to lay anything. We spent about four hours playing games on the computer - I loathed computer games - yet I had a soft spot for flight simulations, so I participated this time. After about four hours, including eating a delicious pasta dish concocted by' the chef' Forrest, he left and we moved on to the massive text-editing/design job of designing THE plane. Unfortunately the original text was destroyed after a series of disk movements damaged it. But upon returning to Canberra I had found an early back-up.

"It's all about bidirectional force resistance," I mumbled sleepily to Alex, and then he would direct.

"You know that, don't you Tom?" towards me, the slumbering lump.

"Mmm..."

At about quarter to six, the sun had risen, and I decided to move to the main building to change. It was light enough to make out the edges of the track, but apart from that it was pretty dark. The main building was dark, and I noticed Bunya was not there. So I turned on the twelve volt light that hung above the mattress, and changed my under t-shirt. Cyber-Shaman - awakened by the light - wandered into the main building.

"Good morning." I said, turned the light off and proceeded out, meaning to go back to Brian's.

"You haven't been at Brian's all night have you?"

"Yeah, Unknown and Alex are there, but Forrest left."

"That's just abusing generosity, you can't abuse Brian like that! I'll have to go and talk to them!"

I changed into my t-shirt, over the still morning air hearing Cyber-Shaman's voice carrying. You never imagine hippies getting angry - was this a credible concept? Yet as I walked back, I arrived to watch Unknown sweeping the building and Alex cleaning the clutter. I picked up a pan and brush and began brushing around the mattress, which yielded a rich bounty of dust and dirt.

After a couple of loads of this, Cyber-Shaman returned.

"Keep on cleaning up and then get out of here, if you stay here any longer you'll just give me the shits!"

Unknown protested, but Cyber-Shaman's bark sent the little pup yelping for a corner.

"Now go and get some sleep, because you need sleep!" We wandered on from Brian's back to the main building where Unknown began talking about plane engines. I took a photograph, as Cyber-Shaman came back.

"You must have gone insane from lack of sleep. Get to sleep!"

But we didn't heed his warnings, and waited at the main building until Forrest arrived. Then Unknown began a monologue on cellular movement - as a working model in modern guerrilla armies. None of us knew what he was meaning and it ended up in a shouting match between the step-brothers. After Alex and I pried them apart, Unknown told me to pick up the disks containing the illicit plane plan. Alex, Unknown and I moved on to a place Unknown called the mill.

The mill was past the Dead Turkey and then down a trail with a sign up saying 'the Elands Company'. Alex and I had to wait at the sign while Unknown went and got the key to the communications room. It was an interesting wait - Alex insisted that we got under a bush, as it was pouring with rain.

Alex had five dollars to his name and I had forty - this was a definite problem. We both decided to call our parent/s and arrange something but before we had a chance to think any more Unknown arrived back with the key and we continued the movement on to the mill.

Down the track, on one side pastures, on the other side a small collection of buildings and then off in the yonder, down in a valley was a barn, which turned out to be The Mill. We arrived and found a one hundred by thirty meter barn, which had been neatly subdivided. As we entered, a white four-wheel drive pulled in.

"It's Bruce," Unknown's face lit up. Bruce was the chief of the technology behind W.F.A. - without him, W.F.A. would crumble and since W.F.A. was a communal group without a leader, I mentally established Bruce as Unknown of W.F.A. Bruce moved quickly and opened the back of the four-wheel drive, and pulled out two large tents. The size of the mill meant that he could do all this under the body of the mill.

Unknown walked up to Bruce as he moved quickly through; unfolding the ripped tent.

"Can we use the communications room?"

"Who's we?" Bruce turned to us, for the first time I met his gaze. He was mid-to-late forties, covered in thick brown beard; five foot seven; clothed in blue overalls, somber, yet sharp, his face recessing to a tension tight forehead. He appeared educated; he had a degree in engineering.

"This is Tom, and Alex," Unknown introduced us. I did the subconscious middle class reflex and shot out my hand, which he shook. Alex slouched off.

"What we need is some technical support," Bruce said. "I can only do so much and it is never enough. We have people out in the forest who take these sea radios and then they come back and their internals are no longer working. It could be anything from a broken crystal to internal shorting; and I have to sit down with each of them and repair them; and move in and out this shit". He waved his hand over the ripped tents.

"It's too much!" Unknown interrupted.

"No, it's not too much," Bruce snapped. "After all, if I wasn't here what would happen? Anyway, this rain had meant that all the camps have mudded up and no one can move."

"I was out there two days ago."

"Yeah, and I was out there forty minutes ago, Unknown!" Unknown was not supposed to interrupt.

"So if you can do any repairs here - and I have heard your speciality is serial communications." I smiled a little.

"See what you can do with the board and anything else you can do would be great."

"Now what's this about the communications room?"

"We want to work on the design of the recon plane," Unknown said.

"Ah, yes, you have spoken to me about this project. The problem with the communication room is that the computer is just a stripped down 286 - it doesn't have graphics."

"We will be using DOS text edit." I spoke for the first time.

"Okay, that should be okay."

"Have I told you about the choppers around the compound? It is just the New World Order coming into play. Have you heard the news from down in Melbourne?"

"No."

"There was a protest about closing Richmond High. And Kennett called in the police, and they just wiped out the peaceful protest. They said that they hadn't seen that much force used since the Springbok tour," "My mother was in that," I added to establish the fact that I had some subversive ancestry.

"Yeah, so was I," Bruce added. "So it is all the New World Order."

"If those subversive hippies get in the way, fuck them up," Unknown laughed.

"Yeah, something like that. Now what you can do for the time being is the tents need unfolding and moving."

We set about doing that, and then Bruce threw us the keys to the communications room and departed. Unknown wandered off, and we were approached by a five foot six, blonde/brown ring-curled female who was roughly twenty.

"Are you going soon?" she asked.

"You want to use the computer?"

"No, it's Unknown, he never stops talking. I haven't seen my sister in six months, and I can't get a word in."

"Okay," we laughed, familiar with Unknown.

That night I slept in Jack and Jill's caravan. There was no meal. Unknown, his brother, Forrest, Alex and another Elandian and were eating in the other end of the caravan; and talking about acid trips taken - a conversation I could not participate in.

Chapter 3

Two days later and I had been left in Jack and Jill's Caravan while I recovered from a bizarre case of the flu. This had meant that I was in a closed caravan, eight hundred meters from the nearest possible homosapien. This virus made me more than usually delirious, and I slept 80% of the time, and spent the remaining time wondering if my friends had returned from the forest. It had been like this after the manic evening of talking about trips. In the morning after, I had a hungry night's sleep. My peers were planning on moving on to the forest (aka Compartment 209) and left at eight in the morning, briefly awakening me, and asking whether I wanted to travel with them. Alas, I was feeling the effects of the flu, and doubted I would be any use.

In this two day period I wrote letters, ate twice and listened to Ice Cube. I had no real indication of events occurring anywhere, but in the fifty meter radius that was Elands. The first morning, at about eleven, I staggered the four kilometers to Elands General Store, the overpriced shop.

The shop had a sign outside saying 'Elands General Store' in fifteen centimeter script and 'COLD BEER' in forty centimeter script. One could expect to pay 250% on Canberra prices, yet I bought some candles, a bottle of THE brand-name cola and a packet of chocolate biscuits - I must have been sick.

I stayed under the alcoves of the General Store, ate my biscuits, drank THE brand-name cola and began writing the text for the Underground Survival Guide about death threats. I was having my ultra-depressed day - and I was juicing it for all I could.

I returned to the caravan with a set of candles - Jack and Jill's caravan had limited twelve volt power than only served one globe in the place - candles were really needed!

And a unit of suet, that I thought was butter - it was a delirious thang! I returned to the caravan and passed out for about four hours. When I awoke, I desperately tried to find some fresh water. I was so feverish, I staggered and fell - inflicting impressive bruises up and down my torso, arms and legs. Eventually I got the water and took two panadols, passed out and woke up about two hours later with a wonderful fever headache which meant I couldn't sleep!

But I had a FACE magazine to keep me company - and what

a wonderful job it did. I had never experienced real physical isolation - intellectual isolation was a familiar friend, something I had dealt with all my life. Emotional isolation and I had partied into the early morning every Friday night for many years. But thanks to my high fever and lack of water and food, over the next couple of days I saw my friends returning many times - I was delirious - and when this was not occurring I wrote letters and stared at my dear friend, the FACE magazine.

On the second afternoon I had been there by myself I wandered outside to get some water. I also needed a shave. My fever had been reduced and I could now actually move without that horrible flu-muscle feeling. I was outside when I heard a voice.

"Tom," coming over the ridge - I couldn't identify the voice - the ridge suitably morphed the sound.

"Yeah," I called out, "I'll just get my shoes."

"Okay, I'll meet you halfway." I still couldn't recognize the voice but I ran inside, grabbed my shoes and returned outside.

"Ah! Tom," said Unknown. "Can I come inside?"

"Sure, would you like some food?"

"Yes, thanks. I need to talk to you."

"Oh, okay," ushering him into Jack and Jill's caravan.

"I have some friends you might like to meet. As I was walking back I walked past the phone and it just rang, and I thought, who is this? So I picked up the phone and it was my contact from Sydney. They have started moving - sweeping the East Coast. It's all the T.L.A. (Three Letter Acronym), they are part of the New World Order, or the Order of the New World, you explain it in your novel. Now what did he say, your friend's score was 43, that means that you are number forty three on their list of dangerous individuals - you know they were watching you last night.

Upon arrival I had found a few of the local Elandians had heard of the evil T.L.A., yet they were already understanding the T.L.A. relationship - this was simple Conspiracy. The logic explained EVERYTHING.

To them, when the social security didn't come, it was the evil T.L.A., when the Police choppers came overhead, it was the evil T.L.A., when locals heard noises in the bushes at night, it was those T.L.A. agents that were up from Sydney. Perhaps I had created a cargo cult of acid-ed-out hippies who needed a folk leader and a prophet. Yet their version of the Conspiracy was not pure 'Barbalet' Conspiracy - they had added something called the New World Order, or as their charismatic leader described it - Order of the New World. So Unknown had a secret movement that he didn't tell anyone about and it followed my fictional ideas introduced in my novel.

Now with the aid of simple cooking implements and Vegemite jars he demonstrated to us the basis of the New World Order.

"The problem we are having is identifying this," he said, shaking a cooking implement.

"It's a potato masher."

"No, it is a specialized team, an international team. They are greater than the T.L.A., but not as high as the CIA. They operate out of the Arctic. My contacts have told me about them - I don't think you would know about them."

The Arctic?

An interesting assumption - had his contacts existed, I might have argued the point. The placing in a true Conspiracist tree diagram would show my novella filtering into control of all Australasia - but since I now disavowed that book, it was slightly different. Still, for someone who had limited practical study of Conspiracy it was a good diagram - though it was completely unfounded - and insane. His belief in 'the Arctic Posse' pointed to his insanity.

"We are dealing with something really, bigger than I think you know."

I couldn't understand what he was talking about - I had created the movement and the fictitious fears of the movement - so if anyone was knowing what was bigger than them, it was me.

Now Unknown was talking about the East Coast scanning. According to him, helicopters had started moving up the East coast. Yesterday they had moved from Melbourne to north of Sydney. Performing a little fast logic, I deduced that the helicopters would have to be traveling at least one hundred kilometers per hour over country areas, and fifty over city areas. It would have been impossible to cover that area and scan all the way for illegal electronic activity - as he was claiming. There were two points here: he could either be testing my psyche or he could have been psyching himself up, and testing my belief in his credibility. He talked about a fellow called the Wizard who would talk in encrypted terms referring to golf. Within these terms, the lawnsman was your author, caddy was an army base etc!

After a little experience with hackers, I knew this Wizard fellow was a bogus hallucination - telephones don't just ring as you walk past them! His contact description was straight out of a fifties spy novel, and was not credible.

"They're what we need; we'll get 22s, and a few AKs..."

I had never seen or used guns. An anti-viral-software-creator's weapon was his mind - it killed whole nations and left executives in their wake. The thought of using a weapon like a gun was NOT what the Conspiracist movement was about. But the fellow who thought I spoke like a prophet, now found a blessing in having firearms! Perhaps he couldn't use his mind.

This scared me, I had come to northern New South Wales for a holiday and not to hear about the Conspiracists and their plans to create a revolution largely based on my book". But slowly, I was finding an un-focused and uncontrolled movement around my book even before publication.

I was pondering what to do, puzzling if I should point out, the fellow was insane. I didn't believe a word of his. To tone down the conversation, I asked him what had happened in the forest.

"Oh, we got out there. And I was doing recon with Alex and Forrest. Forrest was just complaining, and he didn't understand what cellular movement was all about. He always argued, and Alex wasn't much better. So we got to this point where we had to clear a trail, and Forrest said we didn't need to do it, and he wandered off. And he and I had an argument, and I swung a piece of wood and missed Forrest and hit Alex in the head. Forrest had a big fit and punched me in the nose, and I went off and had a bit of a cry. He always uses the same things against me."

This changed things! I guess that eliminated the insane lecture - it gave a slight twist to the Elands existence concept.

"So how is Alex?"

"Oh, he's fine. I left the forest before they did."

Violence equates to immense stress in my mind. If you take a seemingly dangerous situation, and add a little violence - you have a real danger. This was a dangerous situation that I had eleven more days of, and my subconscious was not reacting to typical stimuli - I was in a subtle shock. I had to do some fast thinking: here we had a proven violent individual, who claimed to have access to firearms, who also claimed that he was creating a political movement based on my writing. I had two options - I could either remove myself from this situation - lie low and wander off into the bush with a little food and return occasionally for more food for the next eleven days; or I could move in under this psychologically unstable fellow's wing and win his friendship - which I already had. What I needed was his comradeship. I smiled meekly, and took on an intellectual gaze which I reserved for the occasional mirror I had the misfortune to walk past.

"I know about these people. You are dealing in my realm," he said, shaking the potato masher.

"I don't think you do." I wasn't going to get into a pointless argument about which of us really knew about something that didn't exist. The pause was broken.

"Let's go, I want to introduce you to some interesting people." Moving out into the bracken of the Elandian landscape I assumed it was about seventeen to eighteen degrees. Time here was rather funny actually - you became extremely dependent on the phases of the sun. The walk led us towards Brian's caravan.

"I'm worried about the possibility of T.L.A. agents following us, I know they are in the area, and I think they will interrogate you." At this moment a black-clothed figure jumped from behind some bracken. Unknown flew into what a schlock cliched person would call attack mode, throwing his heavy goggles at the offender and running towards it.

"It's me man," Alex peered out from behind his beanie.

"Very bad timing, man," Unknown snarled. "Tom and I are going for a walk, you'll see us around." We walked to the entrance to the lot in almost silence.

"I think you will like these people. I know they like you. First we need to talk about weaponry."

We walked the kilometer to Jezz's house. Unknown stopped at the gate.

"There's something wrong here, no-one's been here for twenty four hours."

This meant that we had to search every outside location before we went inside - under order of Unknown.

All we found was the track of a bike that had come through after the last rain. I was dwelling rather heavily on his comments about weaponry. We wandered inside and he looked out on the balcony. Inside were about twenty leafed branches of cannabis drying in the late afternoon sun.

"I don't like this," I said pointing through the window at the cannabis bounty.

""What happens if the police turn up and we are in a house with this dope?"

"It's okay, we are just visiting, sit down," he signaled to the sofa in the main room and wandered off into the cannabis drying room, returning back with a branch.

"Would you like some?"

"I'm a anti-viral-software-creator - if I can't remember the system ratios, stripping structures, Wyvern maths, Unipoc and vector memory allocation," I said making a puffing gesture, "it's gone - no-one in this country will know about it - not that anyone gives a fuck about something they don't understand." I smiled at Unknown, who, with scissors in hand, was cutting up the leaves finely into a bowl.

"Yeah, well, there are many different sorts of weapons but in your situation I would recommend a Glock, ceramic, automatic machine pistol," he looked up.

"It's the ultimate weapon, and it will aid you in the revolution - my gift to you for carrying the message." Now as you, my dear reader knows well, the anti-viral-software-creator used their mind, not an Austrian slaying weapon.

"Now that wouldn't be a legal weapon would it? Look, I really don't like guns, but if you are going to give me anything please make it legally registerable."

"You are stupid not to carry a gun; after all the world needs fewer anti-viral-software-creators," he smiled. And what did he know about polymorphism? The more people I met in the Anti-System the more there was peer pressure to carry a fire-arm. My reality was that a firearm would not lead to any of my life objectives. Unknown of our revolution walked on to the stove, and ripped off a sheet of newspaper.

"Here are the weapons I can get, their rate of fire, their capacity, how recommended they are and their approximate cost. While I am working put on a CD."

I wandered over to the CD rack, and selected Public Enemy's *Apocalypse 91* - it wasn't one of their better albums, but I suspected it was a made for CD album that sounded ten times better on the chosen medium - and low and behold I was right.

I wandered back to the sofa and sat down after selecting track (1) 'Rebirth.' Unknown passed me the first piece of newspaper.

"Here are the pistols." I scanned down the list, first coming to the Colt 1911, this was a very reliable weapon - used by the

T.L.A. - but what was this? Guns - these things were romanticized by society. They were used for one thing - to kill people. I was just about to stop this whole scenario and say let's just stop and think, but then my logic kicked in and I realized that if I didn't talk with the fellow, then things could get very dangerous - after all I was out to survive and write a book about this. So I came out with, "Is the Colt 1911 registerable?"

"I don't know."

"The government uses them."

"That doesn't mean anything," I continued down the list. Revolvers? I thought not. Looking down the list of rounds, the smallest was the .22 pistol. It had to be the preferred gift, if he was going to get me anything.

"The .22 pistol looks like me."

"Yeah," he said, passing me the larger piece of paper. They seemed to be the larger arms. AK47s, Uzis, shot-guns - this was an interesting move - here he was just trying to show me the power he claimed to have.

"Come on, we better go," he said, rolling the cannabis into a long joint which he lit as we left. "On to meet your comrades," he laughed. We walked the long track down to The Mill.

Inside three figures sat drinking cask white wine, next to the fire.

"This is Tom, Tom Barbalet," Unknown said.

"Ah," greeted the closest of the figures, a tall fair bearded chap who clutched a guitar and strummed occasionally.

"Would you like some?" a feral lass lifted a glass of white wine.

"No thanks." The third figure was a short slight figure with tightly curled black hair.

"It's like this," Unknown began. "I've received word that the copters have begun scanning for anti-government initiatives, like us! He stared hard backwards and forwards over the four other figures." So anyway, they are mainly after Tom here, cause he's number forty three on their list - if you understand Tom, you understand the state of Australia. I haven't explained to Tom our plan." There was a long pause.

"It is like this: Canberra is the center of this country, you know this," he stared at me, "so our plan is to establish revolution in Canberra. We start by giving all the gangs in Canberra pistols and shotguns; this isn't difficult."

This creates a New Angeles concept - like Los Angeles today, basically this will keep the police busy?" It was a well known destabilizing concept.

"This guy's a smart motherfucker," he laughed, staring again at me. "Yeah, so we give them guns and then we give them the means to get as many guns as they want. Then they clear a neighborhood, and create commune bases. And this keeps T.L.A. busy? And then the revolution happens. Then the world gets better".

In the back of my mind it occurred to me that America would quickly leap on something like this if it happened - and who said that the gang members would want to cooperate with the new government? But here, now, the new Elandian Revolutionary was born.

The curly black haired figure turned out to be a Computer Science graduate - yet he was down with the Elandian Conspiracists. He spoke slowly and quietly, and tried to keep Unknown's eyes on the ground, rather than on the clouds where they stayed.

"Don't worry Unknown, you have really good ideas. Just take your thoughts slowly and write them down, so everyone can get to them," the woman said. She was a typical feral woman, nose ring, dreadlocks and an aging brown t-shirt that was about a size too big and ragged at the edges.

I was just about to take a photo.

"No photos please, I don't care if you are a prophet or not. I better have a shower." She moved off out of The Mill and walked into the distance.

"Never trust anything that bleeds for three to five days and doesn't die. I don't care about bitches, they aren't part of the revolution."

At least Unknown understood the fact that the stereotypical Conspiracist had to believe that females were subversive to the system. I, however, found this quite offensive in reality - I had been raised by my mother solely for most of my adolescent life and I certainly trusted and respected women.

"Better be off, sleep is needed," I stood.

"It certainly is brother," Unknown said, grabbing my shoulder in a sign of respect.

I walked the kilometer back to Jack and Jill's caravan. There I found Alex, sitting rolling a cigarette from old cigarette butts.

"Unknown is sick," I said as I entered, not wanting to say anymore.

"You weren't hit in the head with a piece of wood!"

Good old Alex, you had to give the Understatement of Year Award to him.

"So what did you do?" Alex inquired.

"Oh, I just wandered around and met some people. Pretty boring really. Any food?"

"Sorry, we just have a little bread."

"That's cool, so what happened to you today?"

"Well Unknown had been banned from the forest block. They took a vote after he attacked Forrest and me. Everyone in the community had heard about it even before I returned. I had a long talk to Unknown's mother about it. The community is getting pretty pissed off with him."

"Yeah, I bet. I better be getting to sleep, I feel buggered."

"Yeah, I might too." We both blew out the candles at separate ends of the caravan and went to sleep.

Field Of Chaos

Chapter 4

I woke up in the morning and started a long letter to a dear friend in Canberra detailing the evening's events as Alex slumbered on at his end of the caravan. Then it struck me that this letter may, just may, be read by one of them, and so I quickly burnt the first draft letter, and set about writing another one. I mentioned that Unknown was someone I had never met before, and not Unknown; yet I included the sections about the prophet, and described the other three Conspirators. This was a just-in-case-something-was-to-happen letter.

Things had changed dramatically in the past twenty four hours - and I was in shock.
I sat down and set myself priorities in order of importance:
(1) to survive the remaining ten days;
(2) to remain SANE for the next ten days;
(3) to make sure Alex was not injured; and he, too, left safely;
(4) to try to convince Unknown, that a violent Conspiracy movement would not be condoned by me;
(5) to, forcibly if necessary, get Unknown some form of psychiatric help.

The survival for the next ten days was undoubtedly going to be my main priority. In the past it had not been high on my list of priorities, but I had a hidden adrenaline that kicked in, and added a little excitement to a normally boring life, and this would make a great book. It would be very difficult to remain normal through these sorts of stresses. I had no normalizing influences in Elands, and now I had a group that wanted to protect me, and so would spend much time with me.

Long term, prolonged exposure to insane or actively skew-whiff people would change your expectations of a normal reality - it was what was going to happen. So to correct this, I would need to remember that these people were not solving anything with their actions. I had a duty to protect Alex and so I made sure that I didn't tell any of the evening's affairs, so that he would be safe.

As it was, Unknown thought that Alex was just a weak link in the chain, so he was no longer to be used. I also had a duty to disband this movement as I felt partly responsible for its creation. It was an interesting situation because "these people were part of a familiar genre" to me. I had written in their minds, I knew their thoughts and understood where their weakness lay. There was also a sense of duty in making sure Unknown got some help. It was one thing to have revolutionary thoughts - perhaps it was something that many young people had - but the reality was that he was having hallucinations and that was not good.

And so, I formed a letter, enveloped, addressed and stamped it.

This may be the last thing the outside world was to see of me. My last will and testament.

There was a revolutionary movement arming themselves and I was their prophet - who would be martyred if this was to be my testament. I left Jack and Jill's caravan, letter in hand, when I saw Unknown. My movement froze and then I lifted a hand in greeting. He smiled and walked over and plucked the letter from my hand, looked at it. This was going to be the last moment of my otherwise boring life.

"Who is this to? One of your hacking contacts?"

"Ah, a school friend."

"I can post that for you, I'm going down that way."

What to do, what to do. I had to say fine otherwise he would be suspicious.

"Fine, I'll see you around." Off he walked. I went back into the caravan and collapsed.

Now I was done for. The situation had changed again in a matter of minutes.

Unknown was gone for the next three days: in this period I didn't sleep too well. The realization was that he could be collecting together a posse to push off the anti-viral-software-creator, but I normalized with the idea that it was more likely that nothing had happened. In this time Brian returned. He was like a younger Cyber-Shaman, with exactly the same mannerisms.

On the second morning, I walked to Elands General Store to purchase candles. Also to buy chocolate rations that made up for lack of other things like carbohydrates for me and Alex. I arrived at the store after the half hour walk, only to find the thick curly-haired fellow and the feral lass buying supplies - had Unknown gotten to them after reading the letter? Had Unknown read the letter?

"Buying supplies?"

"Supplies? Oh, yes," he smiled. Unknown hadn't opened the letter! I returned to the caravan. Alex was still sleeping. It had happened that Alex spent most of his evening with Brian and his two companions, playing computer games and smoking cannabis.

Brian's two companions were an interesting sideline, they too had fled Canberra, but for a different reason. These two characters can be referred to as the drug dealer and the heavy. Their presence was enough to make me want to keep away from Brian's building. The heavy was on the run from a restraining order, apparently he had smashed a window with his fist and broken the glass so it hit his daughter's head. He had four children and was in his late thirties. The dealer was considerably younger and of a lighter build. He wore a loose white t-shirt, and under the t-shirt was his black and white rat - which lived on his body. One had to describe these two as mellow characters, unless of course they heard that the police had just searched the dealer's house - then the heavy would fly into a twitching rage where he described how he was going to get his gun and kill the bitch (his wife), if he had to spend another evening in the cells.

Forrest, Alex and I formed a posse, eating and talking together. The big news of the three days was Monday which heralded the trip into Wingham to buy food. The underlying factor of the past week was that we had been living on one and two meals a day - and so food was treated with godlike status.

We sat in Forrest's caravan discussing what we should buy - we had thirty dollars to live on for the next week. Scandalous Alex wanted to spend his money on chocolate and cordial - he didn't eat fruit, never had, and never would. I created a more rational shopping list and we did spend our last four dollars on steak. Alex and I wandered back to Jack and Jill's caravan, where I slept from lack of food: I had only eaten dinner yesterday I hadn't had anything today and it was midday.

I was woken by Alex, who had returned with the box of food. That evening we ate steak. It was quite intoxicating when compared to our life of rice, honey and curry powder. We cooked tomatoes and onions with it, and recoiled in ecstasy at the beautiful textural brilliance of the meat. Unknown returned, and said nothing about the letter. And neither did I. He and I merely exchanged greetings and he disappeared again for five days.

Alex and I became increasingly worried about his disappearance. We heard stories from Forrest: apparently there had been a time when Unknown had taken a lot of really strong acid, in early April, and after this time he couldn't talk for about three months - this could be a great explanation for his behavior.

We also heard word from the general community that Unknown was in Wingham spending his money at a pub, he had $400 for his house, which Alex and I were supposed to be building.

It was a bit of a joke really, a very sad joke.

Five days passed, my flu came back and I was incapacitated by fever and delusion. Alex said that there was no real point in going to the doctor and this was the feeling of the general community - it was against the Elandian philosophy. So the days passed and Alex and I starved. The most enjoyable thing I found was concentrated grape juice, 300mls for a dollar forty. It was cheaper than anything else. And I drank it slowly with plenty of water. Alex didn't like it.

He said the amount I drank would lead to problems, but I pointed to him that it was a better vice than cannabis. When I had bought it I had passed Unknown of W.F.A. he did not say anything to me which was a relief. I suspect he misunderstood my starved appearance for a cannabis intoxicated state.

And he had better things to do. He was being interviewed outside the store by a reporter about alternative cultures. I felt like yelling, "It's fucked, there's no food, and no sanity." But my starvation stopped me from saying anything, as I left. It was a beautiful, sun-drenched Eland morning. The dew glistened on the grass and fern-like bracken. The dense scrub and tall trees echoed with the sound of thousands of small birds. Somewhere in a small damp caravan set in a clearing, Australia's last living anti-viral-software-creator felt depressed.

Unknown had been gone for five days and was waking up in Wingham Park with a fourteen-year-old he had slept with the night before.

Apparently this was a nice feeling - it had to be explained to me, I had never felt it. It seemed bizarre that his enjoyment caused me to feel depressed. Life caused me to feel depressed, so ultimately if Unknown was 'enjoying' a fourteen-year-old - I was feeling like I always felt.

On day five my influenza changed to what I thought was appendicitis. For this reason, I left to find Cyber-Shaman and explain the situation, so when my appendix eventually ruptured, I could be driven the one and a half hour drive to Wingham. I found Cyber-Shaman in the bulletin board caravan, and ended up working there until I returned the eight hundred meters to our caravan at midnight. Surprisingly, the caravan was illuminated. Alex was sleeping? When I entered I saw Unknown had returned and was talking to Alex.

"Ah, a face I haven't seen for a while. Tom, it is good to see you. They have moved in helicopters, I've seen them - we have to move tonight, T.L.A. is in the area. I have a safe location."

My first question - "Does it have food?"

"Yes, plenty." Stuff the pseudo-T.L.A. threat, there was food in dem-dere hills. The walk was described as being four kilometers, it was actually eight kilometers as the crow flies! I packed my pack (40kg) and set out with Unknown. The power of the thought of food was enough for me to think about playing his game for an expected 4km walk. Okay Barbalet, this would really test your role playing ability; there were T.L.A. (agents) in the area. Because I had written about the fictitious Conspiracists view of T.L.A., I knew how to describe crack-night operations by T.L.A. agents.

They stood in skin-tight dark blue (almost black) bodysuits which covered all but their eyes, to which were attached stereo infrared scanners that had LCD over-viewers that used fuzzy logic to provide positive edges to solid heated objects. These pieces of vision enhancement were connected serially to the on-body computer that pinpointed their exact position and gave them instant access to maps and text, and enabled them to take already digitized infrared photos. Apart from this, they had specially modified Colt 1911s. These, of course, had infrared transmitters that made pin-pointing targets highly accurate.

This description captivated Unknown as he finally realized that his mind had created some pretty powerful motherfuckers. So we walked the 8km, and it took from 0100 to 0430. Unknown was shaken the whole trip. I attributed this to the somewhat common mentally ill paradox - he had created something which he subconsciously knew wasn't the truth - and yet, now he had me confirming his creation.

It was a bit nasty of me to do this but it was because I was extremely angry about the lack of normality in this, my holiday. Also in a quasi-analytical way it showed me that he was very weakly insane. To be truly insane he would have walked the path like a trooper and not given a fuck about T.L.A.

Yet this wasn't enough, I had to add one little extra.

"You know why the choppers are here, of course it isn't W.F.A. - it's Defense in the area. They don't want W.F.A.'s scanners working while they do a Defense movement. Mind you this is top of the line information. Do your contacts tell you that?"

"Ah, that was what the bit about the club house was about." This fellow was insane: there was nothing I could do.

"You know an Aboriginal spiritualist told me that no white man would ever succeed in the area."

"Yeah, you told me."

"You know they paid off all the Aboriginal elders in this area $60,000 to say that there wasn't an Aboriginal site in 2-0-9."

"Only $50,000?" I was playing games.

I guess this reaffirmed to him that I knew what was happening and I had true insight (i.e. don't hit me over the head with a lump of wood). When we finally arrived, we lit candles revealing a cat and a corrugated iron walled building. I was wet with sweat and shivering heavily - we needed to make a fire and boil some packet soup - yet he insisted we check the building for T.L.A. bugs and set up traps.

Eventually he passed out - he had little sleep the evening before, primarily because he had been with a fourteen-year-old in a park. I made the fire and the packet soup. He woke, ate his broth and commented that he thought he had been in the park with his broth and with 'his girlfriend'.

He went back to sleep, it was morning.

I thought to myself, why was this motherfucker being so stupid, he had more than I had, he had a fourteen-year-old! And yet he would risk this for a piece of my writing he had never even read - I guess that defined insanity pretty well.

Ah alas, the prophet had to be sans female, sans existence really. It must have been difficult to find a seventeen-year-old, wise, virgin, Conspiracist (or so they thought). Maybe this and the fact that I could string a couple of sentences together, made me a likely person for prophet-dom. Another thing I didn't understand was that if he was a Conspiracist, then why did he believe in love, wasn't he aware of the complete ban against love in the Barbalet Conspiracist movement!

The sun revealed a room four meters by five by three. The building was completely made from corrugated iron. We shared the building with an orange and white tomkitten who had been removed from his mother too early, and so, wanted nutrients from anything it could get its paws on. It was funny, in a closed system, because there were only one of two of us and so mutual introduction was not necessary.

Chapter 4

As far as a good safe house went, this was not perfect at all. The direct vision from most of the main building/room was covered by the same sort of sandalwood that they were logging in the forest - only a few generations younger. They were great for obstructing vision, but the crack-night T.L.A.'s infrared could have ripped through them as seen everything clear as day, that is, had they been real. After photographing my new feline companion, I wandered over to explore the caravan.

Here I found the most homely setting I had seen the whole trip - a clean caravan that wasn't rotting, that actually smelt of something that wasn't rotting food - a sweet, shop-bought, spray on fragrance. Over in the back half of the caravan, behind the bedding was some brain-numbing, intelligence-rooting, keeping-the-working-class-down, soft pornography. I glared at it for about five minutes and then realized that it wasn't running away from my glare. I then wandered from the caravan back into the main building stepping over Unknown to light the stove which lit after much fuss with wood, kindling and paper. I stepped back over the unanimated slumbering body, and turned to stroke my furry companion. Unknown leapt from his slumber standing completely upright and facing me as if to attack, I hid my initial shock and said, "Unknown, it's me. Tom."

He continued to glare, in his patented manic manner, raising his fist. And then slowly you saw the expression of knowing cross from his nose to cover all his face and within a second he body had taken a more reflective pose.

"So, how did you sleep?" I stammered.

"Reasonably". I set about the task of making pancakes with the food items that were available.

"You know many people can't see the point of carrying out the customs of the straight world," Unknown began. "Like things like washing, but you have to understand that washing is crucial. It keeps you clean," this was truly an insight.

"So I wash, like the people do back in the straight world."

We ate our pancakes listening to rap music."

"Los Angeles is really nice, quite violent and confronting in many ways, but it has social structure that I feel comfortable with. You have to understand that Los Angeles is the pinnacle of human existence in Western society, after all, where does all our propaganda come from?"

"Yeah, I guess so. So why were you there?"

"My father was working there with my stepmother who is an American national."

"Oh, I never knew that your parents were divorced, like my parents."

The reality was that the person he called "Dad" was not his father, his father had been a one night encounter, an Italian. The fellow he referred to as being his father, was Forrest's father and had adopted him as his own son.

"My father was doing research on his field, the Emotional Sociology or Sociological Emotionalism - if you like. As you might imagine it is a pretty specialized field. And my stepmother is a medical anthropologist: they were both working at UCLA".

"Of course, you have met my mother. She's a very powerful lady."

"She seems to be."

"Someone I greatly admire. She was originally a trained historian, but became an author and now she protects Australia's interests in Egypt, Libya and the Sudan, and also the interests of her three sons." I smiled.

Chapter 5

We began packing for a day trip, I was to leave a majority of the 40 kg. I set about washing many of my clothes. I had not washed any clothes for twelve days. And Unknown set up a number of traps around the building and caravan, so no evil T.L.A. agents could get to it.

The long walk started with Unknown describing how he had never seen anyone die, but he had seen video footage. It started off being a criminal, then it became a hacker (not much difference?), then it became a Canberra hacker, and then it became a Canberra hacker who was being chased by T.L.A., and the video recorded the last dying minutes of his life. Soon after that the video was exported, and disappeared without a trace - one of his contacts had sent it to him. In reality all I had done was pull together a few sentences, write a novel and thereby create a political movement.

I was walking to our new camp when I was greeted by a small group of local boys. One turned to me and asked; "Who is your father?"

After all, had I been from the community there could have been only half a dozen possible mothers.

"Jack Barbalct, the leading sociological emotionalist, perhaps you have heard of him? I'm not a local."

The eight kilometers continued to tick away. Unknown continued to talk about arming the Elandian Conspiracists.

There were three categories: Urban Warrior, Guerrilla and Intellectual. I had insisted that the third phylum be created because I didn't find myself in either of the other phyla.

The Urban Warrior carrier a modified AK47 (shortened barrel, all metal, with metal stock folded down, it would be under fifty centimeters long) with a modified clip that held sixty rounds, and a long barreled, silenced .22 semi-automatic pistol (intended as a stun weapon). In close combat, the .22 was effective, but close combat training would be useful.

Apart from this, evasion in crowds, in city and suburban surroundings would be crucial. The difference between city and suburban evasion was great. City evasion was based around locating protection and flee points where one must keep eyes moving quickly and look for objects like the corner of buildings and working out the distance, the movement time between your present location and your new location - it also included details like danger and exposed areas.

Suburban evasion was about jumping fences and being able to clear and defend houses, with minimum interference. City evasion was far more mentally tiring where suburban evasion was far more physically tiring. Of course every troop member must maintain maximum physical fitness. Dress had to be loose and baggy. Minimum identity (ID) was to be carried.

The AK47 was an intentionally banned weapon in Australia - it was an assault rifle that was used by militia. You couldn't carry an AK47 unless it was concealable. Modification was made through shortening the gas return pipe as well as the external barrel to minimum specifications. This reduced the range drastically, but it also compacted the weapon.

The Police Departments of Northern America used two terms to describe the damage inflicted by a round (a bullet), the first was the Temporary Wound Cavity and the second being the Permanent Wound Track. The T.W.C. was created by a small fast moving bullet, and it meant that minimum damage was caused and the body merely went into a state of shock after five to twenty seconds. The body's elasticity would quickly contract after impact and restrict the damage. The P.W.T. however, was to create the maximum amount of damage possible and was used to incapacitate instantly or kill. The .22 round could be used primarily for T.W.C. however if it hit the brain or heart, it had the same effect as a P.W.T. round, such as the AK47's 7.62mm round or a 9mm pistol round.

The Guerrilla was the jungle equivalent of the Urban Warrior. They carried sniper or standard AK47s, and a 9mm semi-automatic pistol or a long barreled, silenced .22 semi-automatic pistol.

Apart from jungle combat and close combat skills, they also had advanced survival skills (could last for four days without sleep; could go for a week on one small meal a day and very little water) and basic tracking. The Intellectual was primarily an urban dweller, yet they could survive elsewhere. They carried a short barreled, silenced .22 semi-automatic pistol which was only to be used in life threatening situations.

We moved along the track, which trailed us back to Elands Primary School and the Elands General Store, and kept walking towards the fire station. Opposite the fire station was a popular meeting place for young Elandians who sat around and smoked cannabis in a main room and talked about whatever came to them. I had only ever been there when Unknown was there, and he dominated the conversation.

Today Unknown entered and identified a fellow called Peter, medium sized, solid, red hair.

"Peter, we've been staying at Heifa and Maria's," Unknown said. "Now what has a dumb sucker like you got with calling her up and asking to fuck her? Like she is going out with this bikie; who wants to kill you, and you call her and tell you that you want to root her!"

"Well, I thought it was sort of a compliment," Peter laughed, "I mean I had been hassling them for a while and just thought, she's nice, but she is a bit of a Mustafa."

"Yeah, so she's Greek. I'm not going to protect your arse from the pissed off bikie!"

"Well, it's a bit funny."

"Yeah and he sees it's a bit funny, but she's pregnant and you don't call her up and ask to fuck her."

"Well, Unknown I don't care, just another motherfucker wants to jump me."

"We will just watch."

In the ensuing silence, Unknown passed me a pornographic comic.

"I like this," he said, smiling, "It's about real people, real characters, real adventures."

I stared for a moment at the large-breasted heroine and realized how far from reality it really was. He was a sick boy. My dislike of pornography was something that came from a reverse psychological understanding: it gave a pseudo warmth, but offered nothing deeper. It was sad that men could get enjoyment out of this kind of material - it was dehumanizing. Unknown looked over to make sure I was enjoying it.

I put the magazine down, reached into my rucksack and produced his favorite tape, the House of Pain. He put it in a cassette player and turned it up full blast. From here we moved on to the Dead Turkey Cafe. The Dead Turkey was a great meeting place and it had a Yuppie ambiance that obviously appealed to the greater alternative community - perhaps it reminded them of the coffee shops of their 'youth', back then when they had lived with the System, back then when they had lived in the System, back then when they were the System. Now they could get all that from the coffee shop, without worrying about T.L.A. watching them - or could they? Unknown would have argued otherwise - their Utopia had been destroyed because I had passed on the evil Conspiracist knowledge which had created a movement that had created the fear. Here in the Turkey cafe, Unknown met a fellow who led him back to the phone box. While waiting for the phone our friend with the sister from the mill walked over and spoke to Unknown, her name was Amy. Occasionally, no, actually a majority of the time she would stare inanely at me - it was something I was familiar with, at school, on buses!

Unknown recommended that I continue back to Jack and Jill's caravan. But because I knew there was no food there, it would be wiser to move back to The Mill with Unknown. We set off.

On the way Unknown saw a local selling another local a small 90 cc motorbike. Buying was a chief creation of happiness in capitalist society - after all, you couldn't have political satisfaction, so you might as well have possessions to make you feel better.

Unknown, however, did not see through this - and had a weakness when it came to purchasing. Motorcycle ownership was one of his petty dreams. These locals appeared to be blue collar straights - which was a classic Elandian classification, if ever I heard one. I was left on the track with orders to wait for him. Fuck that. After waiting a minute, I trudged through the meter-high grass to the classic 'straight' Elandian wooden shed building - obviously his house. The fellow who was about to sell him the bike, was a classic blue-uniformed mechanic, the other man, in his late fifties leaned over the bike and asked how much it was for the repairs.

"Oh just a couple of beers."

"What do you drink?"

"V.B., mate, V.B. "

Unknown and I left and moved across to The Mill. Off in the distance, I saw a figure that looked like Alex, firing a compound bow into a mattress lent against The Mill.

Unknown raised his hand, and the figure raised his hand - a mutual greeting, and then there was a run towards the figure. As he came into view I realized it wasn't Alex, but a birdlike figure who shared Unknown's insane glare.

"Good shooting," Unknown said.

"Yeah, it's all in the bow. This one is two hundred pounds, and it's illegal to have it strung like this in public."

"They are dangerous weapons," Unknown added.

"Is he cool?" the figure gestured to me.

"Yeah, he's Tom Barbalet - Australia's last anti-viral-soft-ware-creator - he's down with brothers like us. The fellow smiled and shook my hand. Turning his head increased the bird likeness. We moved inside, and Unknown and the fellow began talking about weapons for the revolution. This man was not a weapons dealer, but a weapons specialist. The conversation drifted from the latest firearms used, to effective sniping, to how to shoot down a helicopter with an AK47.

After a while, Bruce returned to The Mill. He had not spoken to me since we first met. I think he saw I was on holiday and useless to his movement. Unknown walked past me with his weapons specialist and said "I'll tell him about the Defense movement."

"No!" I whispered back angrily, just to make sure he got the message. But it was too late. He began the Unknown rave. I left the conversation as I heard him admit that he didn't know whether it was Air Force, Army or Navy. I wasn't going to stay in this situation, while Unknown inflated his importance with someone else's information.

I started the long walk back to Heifa and Maria's lot. I was considerably shaken. Here was a situation I had to escape from: if I had more perceived information then they would search and find me, and exploit my usefulness. The more interesting scenario was that if Unknown continued to ramble and pointed out to them that I was a high level hacker - not the reality, but his perception - it would cause even more interest.

I was on holiday! That meant forget all worries and relax, or so I believed. It couldn't have been more relaxing than a seven kilometer walk back to Heifa and Maria's lot.

As I passed the Groke Hall, I met the red-headed perpetually stupid Peter and his shorter, younger, even stupider freckled, mate Moss. They were curious to know where I was headed. "Up to that fellow you were talking about's place - with his pregnant Greek girlfriend," Ultimately, I don't think he was familiar with MY sub-tleties. Perhaps he would have understood, "Back to the Greek bitches house, you called her on the phone and asked to fuck."

This would have gone down well. As we walked along, a large male black and white pointer-cross followed us.

"Moss, isn't that one of your dogs?"

"Yeah, but he shouldn't be following us, go back!" he ordered, waving his left hand. He was wearing a jacket and carrying a large pack.

"Yeah, we're going sixteen k' up the road - past you," con-tinued Peter, ignoring the following pointer. Then "Moss, you know we could break his neck. You have plenty of dogs, don't you Moss?" Moss grunted, "Well let's do it. Do they break dogs" necks where you come from?"

"Canberra, ah, no," trying to hide my disgust, remembering where I came from the dogs were called Ben. "Well, let's do it. It is simple. Here, I'll show you. You grab him by the neck and twist."

I think he sensed my disgust.

"I know what he's doing: he's got his Saturday night root up at the Falls, and he's going down to lay his lady." Moss picked up a stick, and kicked it.

I looked at the item and walked past it.

"Kick it!" ordered Peter as if I was some uncultured bastard who didn't understand the stick game.

"Did you ever watch the Smurfs?"

"No, I can't say I did."

"You remind me of Povray, he was one of the knights. He was gay, but he was cool."

This fellow was treading water pretty well. He didn't know who I was or what I did and shouldn't get too off-side with me. Peter was too cocky to be a worry. Although I had a fear that the angry townsfolk would come after the evil hacker who had T.L.A. connections and inflict mortal damage. A majority of the community were capable of being extremely hostile when confronted with a jaguar in sheep's clothing. But these two fools were unaware. I was moving between the two with Moss to my left and Peter on my right. I kicked the stick to Moss and he kicked it to Peter.

We had walked about a kilometer over the twisting mountains.

"Hey, it's good to get the stick occasionally, some people like playing with themselves," chuckled Peter.

"Yeah Povray, stop playing with yourself," continued Moss.

"Stop playing with yourself," laughed Peter.

These people were morons! I sped up my walking and left my 'friends' hitting each other over the head with the stick that had by this point broken in half.

I arrived at Heifa and Maria's just before sunset. I collected the water, talked to Mulray, the cat; disabled Unknown's T.L.A. traps which could have decapitated me with a large pick; and made a fire.

I cooked some more of the cheap packet broth, found the cheap working class sedation material, and the porn in a Picture magazine. Reading an article - the first that I found - Picture compares themselves to the Bible, and claims to be better! The logic? hundreds of thousands had died for the Bible and "no-one was ever killed because of tits". It was a truly intellectual magazine, with a deep political message that really touched your heart. It saddened me really that such things were even available to the masses, and I guess it must have had a market. Perhaps it was the simplicity of the market that saddened me, that ultimately the publisher assumed that all men were so shallow that the only section of their brain that needed challenging was the erotic regions.

The magazine, however, gave me an idea of what the owner of the building was like: a Vietnam veteran who had found refuge in the teachings of Adolf Hitler. His 'literature' was still scattered on the shelves. I poked at it, but it didn't jump back. I went to bed, and the large fire went out overnight.

Chapter 6

I woke and found my feline companion had nestled itself in between my blow-up bed and my pack. My morning was spent creating a garlic based pasta dish and waiting for my washing to dry. It had been out there for two hot days and by midday it was ready. I listened to Pink Floyd's *The Wall*, and a comedy tape that tended to be dope and constipation based - it must have seemed funny to someone, just not to me.

By midday I had packed my forty kilo pack. I had two options, I could either walk the eight kilometers in the searing heat, or I could take the slack chance and wait until about four. I chose to walk in the midday sun with my 1.25L plastic bottle of water, and my image of a Viet Cong doing exactly the same thing - only the Viet Cong had a political reality that he believed in. I was walking so I could get back to block 5 and talk to Cyber-Shaman about means of escape.

I stopped three times on the trip. The last being just after the Elands General Store. By this point every-thing in my vision was white and I was just imagining what a cold ice cream would taste like. That cold creamy sensation with a sweet bite. Ice cream, oh, the ice cream, ice cream, smooth ice cream, ice cream, ice cream with banana, ice cream in a cone, ice, ice cream, ice cream on a stick, ice cream in a tub, ice cream, a tub of ice cream, a huge tub of ice cream. A tub of ice cream big enough to stick your face in. Ice cream.

Before I knew it, I had staggered past the entrance, wandered by Brian's building, moving turtle-like towards Jack and Jill's caravan.

"Man, ah Tom. man, where-you-been?" It was Alex.
"Some food would be nice, some food or some, some water."
"Forrest, could we get this boy some food."
"Not a problem, come back to my caravan."
I dropped my backpack in the bracken and wandered after them. We ate pilchards in tomato sauce. Forrest commented that brine was no good for you, and passed me an orange. Alex didn't eat fruit. I thanked Forrest. Alex told of his adventures and travels to the Falls - the Falls had been on my way, but it would mean another kilometer and, after walking all the way I felt buggered enough.

Chapter 6

On the third last day I was there, a Sunday, 19 December, Alex returned to the colony after traveling to the Dead Turkey Cafe where Unknown had made an appearance. Alex had questioned him briefly about the mysterious disappearing $400. Unknown had said that this was a vicious rumor circulated by the community. Alex pointed out that I wasn't too pleased with him. After returning to the commune he said that perhaps we should go and see him. By this point I was thinking, fuck all this shit.

This would be a show-down between Unknown and me. Slowly Alex and I swaggered up to the Dead Turkey: high noon style. "He's not here," I said, wanting to leave the area as soon as possible.

"I'll wait here." I was a chicken. But Alex had heard the familiar Elandian Revolution tune.

"He's there." We slowly moseyed up to the steps of the Dead Turkey Cafe.

Unknown was there, on the left deck area. We walked over to him and sat down. He raised a hand from the guitar in acknowledgement. The Elandian Revolution tune had developed words;

I know they're coming, There's no use running,
They are coming to get all of us,
They are coming, without any fuss,
Everyone must know, there are no secrets here,
If someone doesn't know give them fear,
But when they come for me, I'll be sitting under my tree,
Yes, when T.L.A. comes for me,
I'll be sitting under my marijuana tree,
We know they're coming, From the forest they are running,
The New World Order is coming in, It's time for the fun to begin,
They all know there's no secrets here,
W.F.A. motherfuckers move out your gear,
But when they come for me, I'll be sitting under my tree,
But when the suckers come for me,
I'll be sitting under my old dope tree."

Alex glared off into the distance, trying to convey as much anger as he possibly could without actually saying anything. I took the half cold ham and tomato jaffle on the table, and ate it.

He stopped the song. I regained some of the blood sugar that would enable me to show anger.

"Perhaps you and I should talk," I snarled.

"Yeah, we should, I have credit - order what you want."

"A cappuccino would be nice," I thought of the warm coffee froth. It would be too good to be true if I could actually have a cappuccino, after all the last time I had coffee would have been at least two weeks ago.

"A cappuccino out here."

"Perhaps I should have a brief conversation, just you and me." On cue Alex wandered off to talk to a small child who was loitering around the main entrance.

"Perhaps we should move out there," I pointed to a table set under the sun.

"Okay," he called in the window, "Could that go out there?"

"Fine," came back. We stood up and moved out to a table and chair beside the road, where Unknown took a collection of cigarette butts out of his pocket and proceeded to roll a cigarette.

"I don't like this, Unknown, I don't like this at all. I don't think you know what you are doing. Your reality is not my reality - you can stay in Elands as long as you like, I have to return to Canberra and if you play games like this, other people will want to play too, pretty soon you will have T.L.A. on your back. When people in Canberra get their hands on this, they won't give a fuck about you - you're already going down my brother. I don't want to have anything to do with you unless you get your priorities right. Number one on your list; don't fuck with me, you have a fourteen year old for that. Number two, if I tell you something - don't fuck with the knowledge - don't play with it, don't twist it. If I tell you something - which I'm not going to be doing anymore, you better remember one thing, I write fiction - reality is described but it is they way in which I do it that has created your movement."

"Look, I had to tell everyone. I had to tell them, because I've been followed, I've been met - like you." The only people who would follow him would be psychiatric staff.

"Let me give you a scenario."

"The Wingham Paper reads: *Mysterious Defense Hacker Warns Greens: Get Out Of 209*" "It did? How did they find out so soon?"

"No, Unknown, it's just a scenario. And suppose you assume I went and saw Bruce, what would he say?" "Look, let me tell you one thing, I did nothing to implicate you. He doesn't know who you are," "No, he doesn't know who I am. He thinks I'm a Defense hacker because that is what you told him."

"I did?"

"And you can't even remember what you said, can you?"

"I can!"

"No you can't! Did you mention the Army, Navy or Air Force?"

"No."

"You did, I heard you."

"Did I?"

"Unknown! Some of the community think I'm a Defense hacker, some of them think I'm an T.L.A. agent! This is because the community doesn't like you particularly, and you thought you would increase your standing in the community by creating a story - or more importantly padding out a story. Now I was not just here on holiday, I also came here with a certain amount of knowledge and I was planning a third book."

"I knew you where working on something."

"Unknown," I said, calming my tone, "You've seriously fucked up, but this will do nothing to you. I, however, stand to lose everything. You see, I trusted you, which perhaps was a little naive on my part, and you fucked up, and now you have lost my trust."

"But there are no secrets in this community."

"Unknown, no secrets? What are you talking about, you are not a leader, you are a tool for the community. You desperately want the community's support and they refuse to give it to you, because you have stuffed up and lied so much that no one trusts you anymore."

There was silence, and Alex walked back.

"Can I just say one thing man? Look, the whole community thinks that Unknown has gone stark raving mad. I still trust you, but if you keep this up, I'm going to have to change my mind."

"The community's fucked, the sooner I get away from these fucking hippies the better."

We all returned to Jack and Jill's caravan, and sat down. Alex was angry because no-one had told him anything, and he saw there were many things that he was missing out on. I pointed out to him that Unknown had stuffed up and told the whole community that I was a Defense hacker.

But Unknown wanted to take the floor, ignoring Alex, he raised the point that T.L.A. had only started harassing him since he met me, and what is more, many of his (fictitious) contacts had stopped communicating with him after he met me. The problem was I was blaming myself too, but for a different reason; I felt guilty that I had introduced him to Conspiracy. Finally, to try to discourage his Conspiratorial mind, I asked him if he believed I was a Conspiracist? He was silent. The correct answer was that I was a Pessimistic/Utopian. Yet I left the question unanswered to make him think about what was happening. Things were beginning to wear on me. Unknown was re-detailing his planned assault and escape from the T.L.A. entrapment, in Jack and Jill's caravan. It seemed strange that within a week he had moved from the T.L.A. being the all seeing, all knowing body - to the true Conspiracists belief - it was all T.L.A.

The more time I spent with him, the more I felt sorry for his twisted mind and the fact that he romanticized my lifestyle.

To me, I could not see enjoyment. Unknown wasn't interested in learning polymorphism. And this was all I had. Perhaps he would have liked to walk the Earth and live my life. I was an emotion hardened man. "Tom Barbalet - Australia's last anti-viral-software-creator and he still can't get a date." I was starting to wonder what was happening.

Something I had written to escape from a stressful and bludgeoning situation, had caused a fellow - who sure he was unemployed, but he had more than I ever could possess: charisma, looks, a fourteen year old - to see a real conspiracy.

What I had was knowledge and that wasn't valued in this country. I appealed to him to stop his militancy - it was without point.

The reality for him was that he could live in Elands and build his house and probably marry any of the local girls, settle down and have a family. Where were his dead contacts? What was his reason for taking arms against the system? Perhaps he saw me as an extremely strong figure and he wanted to imitate this. I shed two tears for the soul of this insane motherfucker and continued. What was he doing? Had he lost any friends - had any of his friends been killed? It was a simple insult to me and the contacts I had had.

To take on my emotions and my thoughts and use them as his own thoughts? He assumed I was a shallow fool. He didn't have the maturity that I had found through the productive criticism of my peers. I found that his immaturity was the biggest insult. How dare he talk about being followed or being met. His reality was not this - he lived in the middle of nowhere. The fool did not see that messing with me through this method meant that he was in twice as much danger - twice as much danger from nothing was still nothing. He had starved me for days, he had abused my intelligence, he had not protected my welfare, he had lied to me, he had told nearly the whole town that I was a high level hacker - possibly with T.L.A. This fellow was just a bastard.

Yet I kept my cool, perhaps because I knew that I would survive. You see I thought like an honorable mercenary - I would work for the System, I would work for the Anti-System. As long as the final result was the same. The first principal was not to break the law, because if you broke the law you were a simple criminal. Fame? No. I just wanted normality and a rather cool understanding of reality, and if a book or two were published, so be it. I didn't care about the Conspiracist Movement.

Chapter 7

Things simmered down. We had a guitar with us, given to us by Amy who was writing a book about the forest. She was very curious about who I was, and what I did.

Rather than ask me, she went to Unknown and asked.

"Who is Tom?"

"He's a friend of mine from Canberra."

"He seems very quiet."

"Yes, he keeps to himself."

"What does he do?"

"He's a student."

"Yes, but what does he do?" Unknown didn't answer, but reported back to me that perhaps she was an T.L.A. infiltrator. She had lent Unknown her guitar: it must have been bugged. Great joy was had in this fact at Play-Guerrilla School.

It was getting dark, I needed to call my mother. Wandering the now highly familiar walk from Jack and Jill's caravan to the BBS caravan, I arrived and found the board whirring through its usual processes. I called directory assistance to get a reverse charges phone call to my mother who was now in Adelaide for Christmas. The first call did not get through. Australian Telecom offered to call me back when they could get through. It was just getting dark, so I sat at the Bulletin Board, until the eventual call.

Talking to my mother normalized the whole situation so much. This was my third call 'home', and it was just a wonderful feeling knowing that there were other people out there. Mum had developed the film I had sent, and now had Cyber-Shaman, Unknown's mother, Alex and Unknown, all together in her hands.

"Unknown looks really seedy," my dear mother said.

"I wouldn't say things like that mum. Unknown was fooling with the answering machine, and all this could be recorded."

"Don't play with me."

"Just don't make comments like that. I'm his guest. There could be problems with me getting to Wingham - I don't know what will happen. Unknown has a trip lined up tomorrow and we stay in Wingham for one night, and then I catch the bus in the morning. It's a party."

"A party?"

"Don't worry, I'll sleep in a back room or something while this party happens and walk to the Big Oyster, where I have to catch the bus. The other option is to go with Cyber-Shaman."

"I'd go with Cyber-Shaman. Has anything happened about Unknown's house?"

"What do you think?"

"Give my love to all the relations. I will call you from Sydney."

When I returned Unknown was bored, his revolutionary form twitched. I suspect that he thought I saw through his lies, and this induced a mutual fear. I knew what he was capable of: enough physical violence to seriously disfigure me. (Even more so!) Yet to him, I was an unknown quantity - there was something about being a quiet mystery - something which certainly worked for me. I was someone who could survive for a year against things that he knew he would crumble under. His thoughts could have been two-fold, perhaps he saw that I must have had a large organization behind me (maybe even the evil T.L.A.) and secondly, he knew that I had many more contacts than he could ever have. I was Australia's last anti-viral-software-creator and I had known the world's first anti-viral-software-creator, a showing of the caliber of contacts I kept, and so if anything happened to me, the person inflicting the harm would have to deal with a bleak future.

The reality which he hadn't fathomed was that it was my trust in God that kept me alive - something he didn't have. So what did I know?

"Could you interrogate me?"

"What?"

"You have had to deal with T.L.A., interrogate me, like they would interrogate me."

This was an interesting predicament - he might as well have asked me to have sex with him - interrogation was merely a mental wrestling match.

It struck me that he was incredibly unstable and it would be possible to force a breakdown if I could interrogate successfully. If he had a breakdown he would have to seek help - and we might be able to spend our last couple of days having a holiday. An obvious problem, I had never been interrogated by T.L.A.

But I could use a little creative license and imagine an T.L.A. interrogation. This was slightly twisted, and rather unnecessary, but it was Play-Guerrilla-School. I began.

"Could you start by describing to us your movement in the past five days?"

The correct response to this question was, "Get bent T.L.A. motherfucker," but his response only confirmed his naivete.

"Five days ago, I left here, and traveled to Wingham to repay debts. In Wingham, I found you [T.L.A.] had fucked with my bank account - you have been putting money in. You are trying to fuck with my mind. Here I'll show you," he reached into his wallet and removed bank slips at a machine gun rate.

"You see?!"

Actually I didn't, I was having trouble reading the slips in the candle light and anyway, all they said was that he had withdrawn four hundred dollars, and mysteriously there had been a deposit of two dollars, obviously interest.

"You see ?!"

"No - actually I don't."

"Anyway, I went into the forest, Compartment 209. Here I met some friends and they had some really good Thai hash and amazing buds."

"You are referring to cannabis resin originating from Thailand, and the flower of a female cannabis cannabis plant which contains more than four percent tetra-hydra-cannabionol, consumption of which is illegal in this state, resulting in four years in gaol."

"They showed me their weapons: they carried nines that could blow you away."

"I'm not at liberty to discuss the weaponry we carry."

"And, you know, it was just a typical conversation." He waved his right hand in a circle.

"I don't."

"And then I got a lift into Wingham with them, and it must have been before twelve, and they were just setting up for a Christian Parade. And I met some people, some friends."

"Could you describe them?"

"Ah, well there were two of them, they are - what? - seventeen I guess, they live in Wingham and have a baby, and with them was Moss. So we wandered under a bridge where we smoked some more buds, and then we spent some time there talking, and this must have been about four hours since I arrived and it was getting dark."

"How inebriated were you?"

"Not very."

"Yet it was getting dark at four in the afternoon?"

"No!"

"Four hours after twelve would be four: now it is not common for it to get dark at four in the afternoon. How inebriated were you?"

"I really don't pay any attention to time. Anyway, I met a group of friends and one of them was this girl."

"She was fourteen. Sex with a minor is an imprisonable offense."

"But she looked older."

"Describe her."

"Well she was short, had black hair."

"I run over things like that; that isn't a human, that's a terrier description. Perhaps her face."

"Shoulder length black hair, very pretty,"

"Was she mature for her age?"

"Yeah, very well developed for her age."

"When did you first meet this fourteen year old?"

"Ah, at a party, a while ago."

"And you didn't want to have sexual intercourse with her then?"

"No, she was tripping with a group of her friends."

"When you say, "tripping", you mean under the influence of a hallucinogen, an offense?"

"Yeah, mushrooms. And she seemed pretty old for her age."

"But she was still fourteen and severely inebriated, I put it to you that you took advantage of this girl and had sex with her while she was under the influence of a number illegal chemicals."

"Not this was early."

"You did this to her multiple times?"

"No! We were talking about the party when I first met her."

"I've moved on from that time, I am taking you to Wingham Park, when you had sex with this minor whilst she was intoxicated. Do you think this was meaningful? Do you think that she has any lasting commitment in maintaining a relationship with you, or was it just the fact that she was severely intoxicated, and the fact that you were larger than her no only in age and mental stature, but also physically. Not only are you a pedophile but you are also a rapist!"

"No," Unknown was trying to hide his fluster.

"Not only did you rape her, you also impregnated her with

your sperm, due to a simple fact that the prophylactic failed to work. You gave this fourteen year old a child. Do you have any means of supporting a child?"

"No," "Let me put this another way, do you have the means emotionally, mentally and financially to support two children, one of which will contain your genetic information and one of which will be the mother of your child, who no doubt will be twice as emotionally fucked as you. I put it to you Unknown, that rather than creating a political movement which you do not hold the mental strength to maintain, you concentrate your energies in raising your new family."

There was a deadly silence. I don't think he really understood what interrogation was about. It even installed a sense of fear in me, that I was capable of reducing a human being to this sort of state. I smiled and asked, "Have you had enough?"

"Ah, yes, it was, interesting."

I suggested perhaps we should move from Jack and Jill's Caravan to The Mill where we would find the girl who owned the guitar.

After some persuasion we moved on. Arriving under the cover of darkness, Unknown explained to Alex and me how there were no secrets. I pushed the point that he was contradicting himself and in fact there were plenty of secrets. All the nations of the world were based on secrets. Amy was at the mill, with her boyfriend, a slow but thoughtful hippy who had been making Christmas decorations for a huge Christmas tree that they were going to create out in the forest. Her boyfriend was bathing.

Unknown said he would make chapattis. But then he spent all the time talking about how W.F.A. was a fucked organization. We were all hungry, so occasionally I would call out.

"Ah, chapati boy - chapati! chapati!"

Eventually I got up and began working on a soup, which meant that I had to clean all the rotting lentils out of a couple of thousand pots - hippies actually ate that shit? - and the mysterious white chunky stuff that smelt like a cosmic collision between yak vomit and curdled milk. There was a full cooking facility, you just had to be ready to wash a thousand items to get to it, and then you had to stoke up the fire. But tonight there was already a fire going which you could use.

"Ah, chapati boy - chapati! chapati!"

I got busy with the 'herbs' and vegetables that were available and made a killer soup - just in time for about ten 'troops' who had just come in from the forest. The evening was spent listening to Unknown's inflated and fictitious stories. Such features included, Unknown goes to sea on a fishing trawler and meets pirates, Unknown survives in the middle of the Simpson desert with just an AK47 for five days and the worst and most daring story of the lot, Unknown survives in Canberra. Later Alex and Unknown headed back to Heifa and Maria's while I walked the more sensible distance to Jack and Jill's caravan.

Next morning I met Unknown at Brian's house. He was talking to the Elands gun dealer.

"So I'm thinking of buying a 200 [cc] or something that can take the road and be run through the bush."

"Have you met my friend, Tom?"

"No, but I've seen him around, how long are you up here?"

"This is my last real day here, I've been here for sixteen days, and tomorrow I head down to Sydney."

"Elands is a pretty nice location."

I looked into this fellow's sparkling deep brown eyes and reflected on the story I had heard about him being on the run from the police. Apparently old Fri, who owned the Elands General Store had told the police that he was in the area, and he had spat in her face. But that didn't matter, it was all the way he looked. He wandered off to talk to Brian.

I was left with Unknown. "You know I can get a copter for

$10,000! A real Russian military one," signaling to the gun dealer, "He knows a guy who is importing them, and Chinese APCs. What he does is import them in three standards, the first is barely running, rusted, needing a lot of repairs; then he has them running well, just with all the armor removed; and then you can buy them with armor, just no arms."

This looked like something 'the crop' would buy.

Unknown continued to repeat himself, maybe four or five times and then I directed the conversation towards arms sales in Eastern Europe, as a change of pace. This merely created another monologue.

I inched away and wandered off to meet Alex at Forrest's caravan. They were talking about the hot conversation that had hit all of Elands and everyone thought exactly the same thing: wasn't Unknown such a fucked individual. Alex and I blamed the acid, and Forrest pointed to the fact that he had lied and 'scammed' the community so much that everyone hated him. After eating at Forrest's I returned and invited Unknown to come over to Jack and Jill's to talk about the world and the movement. After all he was headed for Canberra in the New Year with guns and militants, and there was nothing I could do.

So I decided to part with minimum hassles. I handed him four pieces of paper, three identical which read:

Tom Barbalet
FREE service Espionage consultant; governmental, commercial or underground

And one other one which said *"Amy, Unknown told me that you were interested in what I did. I have been up here working on my third book. If you are interested in knowing what is really going on here, drop me a letter. I'm interested in hearing about your book."* I passed Unknown the papers. He read all four, looked up and smiled.
"I knew you had something going on."
"I always have something going - I'm an anti-viral-software-creator not a prophet, but I have a persona to keep up."
"Now look brother, you better just cool down over Christmas, get some stuffing into you and some relaxation. Your grandparents want to see you, so you better go and see them, it will do you good."

And after a brief discussion, he left and storm clouds covered the sky and a wall of water began to fall.
Alex returned, and we found ourselves wet and stranded.

I had an idea, to get rid of the mosquito larvae that had filled our drinking water for the past sixteen days, not to mention the cooking oil. We should tip the water barrel out. Alex called out, "wait for me," but it was too late, the barrel was tipped and my fingers were attached to the rim. The initial sensation was that of being pulled down, and then the shock that the barrel was going to hit the caravan. Luckily by this point it had lost much of its seven hundred kilo weight. I pulled back my hands and they were covered with blood. I ran back into the caravan.

I had shredded the inside of four of my fingers. The only bandage was eight hundred meters away. I had to run it, but Alex came with me. We arrived at Brian's, I was bandaged and then we set off to the main building. We arrived at the main building wet and blooded.

Cyber-Shaman was sitting at the fire, looking very wise and like a shaman. A plan was made. I was to sleep at Forrest's caravan and when the rain stopped, go and pick up my packs, move them back to Forrest's and sleep until my departure which was at 0530 the next morning. The only problem was that all my clothes were wet and I had a blanket wrapped around my waist.

I slept and at midnight when I woke, Alex was still at the main building talking to Xyan-Dytos, the fabled second cyber-shaman; best friend of Cyber-Shaman. Xyan-Dytos believed in chaos, he obviously hadn't heard of the viruses I fixed with software - I tried to point out that chaos was limited, but he pulled age/rank on me, and we ended the conversation like that. Only a fool with a weak argument would pull an age rank on someone.

My clothes were damp, but I knew that there would be dry clothes at Jack and Jill's. I returned to Jack and Jill's to find that the roof had collapsed with the weight of the water and my clothes were all wet. I returned to Forrest's caravan and slept.

Chapter 8

I awoke at five thirty - the prearranged time. Expecting to be woken, but finding no-one else was up, I moved my two bags from the caravan to the main building. It was 5.45am and I was beginning to worry.

Suddenly there was movement in Cyber-Shaman's caravan - it was Unknown's mother - running from the caravan to the caravan. She arrived there, opening it, only to find that I was behind her.

"Ah, Cyber-Shaman's just getting up. The alarm clock didn't work." I wandered over to the main building and loaded my two packs on, and started the trudge. Cyber-Shaman quickly caught up, and apologized for his alarm clock. We came to the junction were the tracks verged above and below the BBS caravan. Here a neatly cabled fence made it nearly impossible to move under the fence with my pack. But after about two minutes of struggling I finally got under it. It was a limbo event.

We trudged on to a large van and drove across the pass to Hughes' hovel. Hughes was still asleep. Cyber-Shaman ran inside, woke him and then we connected a trailer on the back of the van - they were later going to Taree picking up building supplies. We moved out of block 5.

The ride to Taree was a welcoming revelation. It was dawn, and I hadn't seen the trip in daylight. It was one of the most beautiful areas I had ever seen in Australia; lush, sub-tropical mountains working down to completely level green pastures. We went through Wingham which looked considerably larger in daylight.

But after an hour and a half of driving, we arrived at the Big Oyster. Australia had an obsession with Big objects, I guess Big attracted tourists, and it made up for real tourist attractions. Opposite the Big Oyster was a park dedicated to a fellow - a winemaker - who had the nick-name 'Plonky'. The park was called Plonky Park. Taree was the center of the universe when it came to hot tourist attractions. The Big Oyster was also known as Vienna World, which was a brilliant excuse to have a scantily clad pseudo-Germaness, holding a flagon of lager. We pulled as far away from the Oyster as we possibly could, and opened the van.

Hughes turned, "Anyone for coffee?"

"Thanks," came twice, from two different figures.

We went into the Vienna World supermarket and purchased three coffee-machine coffees. And then we moved back to the safety of the van where my companions rolled sativa cigarettes - in front of the Big Oyster? Far be it for me to argue.

I wandered over to the driver's side, where Hughes was sitting with the door open. Cyber-Shaman was in the passenger seat.

"Cyber-Shaman's been telling me your mother works for F.L.A.! (Four Letter Acronym)" Hughes laughed. The Unknown rumors to induce fear and secrecy had worked all too well.

"No, she works in Foreign Affairs and Trade. She just has security clearance."

"Oh," Hughes continued, laughing, "Perhaps we should have barred you from the area."

"Perhaps you should've," I laughed.

"Canberra is a pretty screwed place. I lived there for most of my life and spent the rest of my time getting out of it. I even spent time in jail there," laughed Hughes.

I stared, in middle-class shock. Here was a really nice fellow, who had spent time in jail - but for what? My logic said that it was probably a cannabis offense. This induced a sense of sadness that these people had created their own Utopia - tangential from the System perceived Utopia - and by creating this Utopia they made themselves open to prosecution by the System. To them, enjoyment was to be loving to people around them, smoking sativa and spending time in forested areas. The System's Utopia was to be as rich as possible and it didn't really matter whether you were rich, or whether you had love - because money could buy location and it certainly could buy love. And who needed sativa when you had more System-correct drugs?

"So you'll be coming back after Christmas?" Cyber-Shaman looked out from the other side of the van.

Poor Cyber-Shaman! I had become remarkably fond of him. He was a very endearing person and had mannerisms that made him a very individual character. Yet he thought I had become one of them - a realization that he had obviously formed in his mind after the weeks I had spent with them and repaired power supplies. It was a compliment, both in the fact that he was offering to let me be part of the intellectual cyber hippy brotherhood but also a personal compliment on my role-playing ability. The fact that although I had had a twisted and sickening holiday, he thought I was enjoying myself, stopped me in my tracks. "Alas, I have to return to school, but there are still holidays," I smiled back.

"You know you can call the board. Try logging on and mailing and play around with it a little. What's your speed? 2400?"

"It will probably be 14k."

"14k, oh, well we'll leave you here."

"Not a problem, see you round!"

And with this, my last connection with Elands apart from the fact that I hadn't washed for sixteen days was over. I looked like an Elandian. I had become one of them in physical appearance.

The bus arrived an hour late and I left Taree headed for urban reality.

I arrived in Sydney with a slight cold and rather malnourished. I had lost 10 kg. Shelter came in the form of a friend of my mother's Bondi Junction flat. It came complete with a copy of Salt-n-Pepa's 'Push It,' the first rap track I had ever heard.

The realization was that in less than a month Unknown would make his way to Canberra with guns, and I still wouldn't have a girlfriend or be a normal teen. But I was Australia's last anti-viral-software-creator, and this had now made me a powerful pawn in 'the revolution': the prophet of the Elandian Conspiracist move-ment. I flew to Adelaide for Christmas with my brothers and my mother's parents. I was hugged and fed every day.

Yet again, I feared that eternal fear of mine, that somewhere, someone was touching someone they loved and I wasn't.

Epitaph

About twenty five years later, astonishingly, I met Unknown again. He and I had been completely isolated geographically. I'd left the country. I had spent many years away, totaling more than twenty years that I had not been in the same country as him. It was quite the experience to sit down with him over coffee in a public place and have a conversation with him. It was really a luxury. It was a luxury that seemed to completely remove the lives that we had both lived.

He started by saying that the first thing they ask you when you enter a mental institution is whether or not you have superpowers. If you admit that you have superpowers, then immediately you are classified in a particular fashion. I thought about this quite strongly. If anyone had superpowers through this, it was Unknown and it was me. We both had superpowers, which we couldn't acknowledge. I smiled a little at this notion of being quizzed about your superpower abilities when you enter a mental institution.

Our discussions became very practical. He was curious what had happened to me, I was curious what had happened to him. I was curious what had changed, associated with the jungle. He said after my departure, things had gotten considerably more militant, vastly more firearms had come in, and more people that had no notion of the area had been a party to this thing.

He also thanked me profoundly for my writing had provided a narrative for him. He could return to my writing and reflect that perhaps revolution was not the thing that he needed to be concentrating on. There are other subtleties, other nuances, but the importance of having stuff written down was something that he kept on saying.

This thing that I had done to come in, to document, to leave, and to provide the documentation after the fact. To educate people for many years about what had happened in the jungle. What the process was there, and also my general observation and interaction, this was a very important thing for him.

I reflected very strongly when he said, "I learned after a period of time that I wasn't really about the revolution. I wasn't about any kind of violent upheaval. I was just an observer myself. What you observed and what I observed, these were just observations worth noting. But to motivate people to violence, to motivate people to make changes, this was ultimately not what we were there to do."

I smiled thinking about that. He had manifest in words and descriptions my own philosophy. The nature of that time was so far removed from where I was now. To come back and see an old friend, see that he had survived. He wasn't in prime physical condition. None of us were after this period of time. What had happened through this time is that he had just grown to know himself in a very different way. His experiences had been very much based on the area he was in and his abilities. He had no means to leave. He had no means to see other things, but certainly he had taken account and he had found other like-minded folk. Other folks willing to engage in discourse and to build and develop the ideas that he had embodied so strongly in my early experiences with him. *It was just wonderful to spend time with my friend.*

To look upon him now, us together, two men entering middle age quite comfortably with the view that we had paid some of our dues many years ago. We had done the things that we both smirked about. This wasn't necessarily all positive; it certainly wasn't all negative. But it was so far removed from the contemporary narrative as to seem so dated. We looked at each other in somewhat embarrassed setting associated with various changes that had occurred in our own existences.

Epitaph

While I was a married man, living my life in a different country, he was still very much his own self. He was still very much someone who could drive a group of people into a series of different discussions and conversations and ideas. He was someone who instigated conversation, who instigated thought, and this was wonderful to see still existing.

Unknown had followed me as much as he possibly could. He had been engaging and seeing where I had continued to write. He was following my work in a very creative and profound sense. He still agreed with my vision, even as my vision had changed. That he still agreed with the people that I brought into conversations, even as these people had changed over time. This ability for him to still pick up my work passively, to not actively be involved, but still be observing it, gave me an immense sense of peace. It gave me a sense that I could continue with what I was doing and he would continue to be a happy observer. Just tapping his finger occasionally, following what I was doing. That was the nature of our friendship. That was the nature of our interaction and our existence.

Just as quickly as we had the conversation, as quickly as things had started, he excused himself and disappeared. He was gone and that was that. That was how it ended. He left me a scrap of paper with an email address and a telephone number. But none of these things worked. This was just his life.

9 7 9 8 3 3 0 2 8 1 2 6 8